Boring, Boring!

Written by Jeanne Willis
Illustrated by Jess Mikhail

Sid was at Nan's.

"Do your homework," said Nan.

"No, it's boring," said Sid.

I have to do a talk on dinosaurs.
Draw a dinosaur, then.
DINOSAURS

"Play astronauts, Nan!" said Sid.
"No, I am doing the laundry," said Nan.
"Get on with your work!"

"Whoops, my drawing has torn!" laughed Sid. "Never mind," said Nan. "Make it into a jigsaw."

“This jigsaw is boring,” said Sid.
“Make a model dinosaur then,” said Nan.

“What with?” said Sid.
“Work it out,” said Nan.

It's snowing, Nan! Come and play snowballs with me.
Sorry Sid, I have lots of work to do.
DINOSAURS

Nan did the laundry.
It got dark.

Where was Sid?

Nan put on her shawl.

She went into the garden with her torch.

What's that in the corner?

It's very tall, with big jaws and claws …

"Do you like my Snowysaurus, Nan?" laughed Sid. "You said to make a model!"

“It made me jump! Make a small one next time!” said Nan.

“Boring!” said Sid.

"I will tell you what's boring," said Nan.
"Doing the laundry."
She hid by the wall.

Good shot!

"Why did you do that, Nan?" asked Sid.
"Because you said to play snowballs!" said Nan.